Introdu

This book is designed for people who are .... and becoming a self employed gardener. I went through this 7 years ago and will talk you through all of the stages, from deciding if it is something that you really want to do, getting and keeping customers and maintaining a thriving and well established business.

Should I Start A Gardening Business?

This should be the first question you ask yourself. I will outline all of the positive and negative arguments and you must go through them , and at the end, make an informed decision about whether or not to go for it. This section aims to make that decision easier for you to make. I started my gardening business at the end of a fixed term contact for my local council, I had no mortgage and no family to support so I did not have a lot to lose by setting up. This will be a much more difficult decision for anyone that is in a steady job and has financial commitments. If this is the case, you could try to start slowly and get a couple of weekend customers to try it out for a few months. You may then decide that it is not for you and then you still have your old job to fall back on, but if you like it, then you could try and reduce your hours in your old job and gradually increase your gardening time. If you start at the right time of year then you will be surprised, as I was, just how quickly you will have enough customers to fill your diary.

I will start with what I think are the positives to becoming a self employed gardener.

- You are your own boss – While you will still have customers that will be telling you what to do, this is significantly different from having a boss telling you what to do.

- Work as much as you want – You set your hours. For the first year you will probably just want to be taking all work that is offered, but once you are well established then you can work the hours that you want to. If you want to work at weekends for some extra money then there will be work available for most of the year for you to do this. If you want to take some time off in the afternoon to pick up your kids from school then it is your decision alone to to this. It can take some time before you become confident enough to turn down work or to leave gaps in your schedule, but you will soon realise that for a good gardener, there is always work available. Being a self employed gardener is also a great job for when it comes to retiring. You can reduce your days as you get older and more financially secure and just cherry pick the jobs that you enjoy to carry on with at maybe one or two days a week.

- Getting paid for what you do – The harder you work and the more you work, the more you get paid. This is not always the case when you are working for someone else. Many employees complain about working more hours than they are contracted to do and not getting paid overtime. This will not happen to you as you set your hours and your prices.

- Set your own price – You are in control of your own income. If you think that you deserve or need a pay rise then you can make it happen.

- Work for nice people – One of the biggest benefits of being self employed is that you can pick and choose the people that you work for. If you don't like someone for whatever reason, then don't continue to work there. There will always be other jobs and you can be getting paid the same for working for someone that you like. I work for some people that I now consider to be friends and it is always a pleasure to see them every week. On the other hand, I have also worked for the occasional person that I have not quite got on with for whatever reason and the occasional customer that is determined to get their money's worth or over critical of the work. I do not think that it is worth working for these people no matter how many hours they want you for. I have known other gardeners to complain about a customer, saying that they are always blaming them for plants that die or that the work is not up to much but they continue to go because it fills 3 hours a week. In my opinion it is not worth it and you should do all you can to replace them. The same can also apply to particular jobs, for example you may not like weeding, eventually you will get to a stage in your career where you will be able to turn down weeding jobs in favour of jobs you enjoy more.

- Fresh air – You are outdoors all year round by the very nature of the job. On a nice summer's day you will wonder why you kept working in that windowless stuffy office for so long when you could have been out gardening all that time. Most gardens will be lovely places to work and you may get to see some wildlife that many do not, for example I have had a robin land on me a couple of times while I have been weeding.

- Money – While gardening is a very rewarding job, you are thinking about doing this because you want to earn money. The money can be good if you get your pricing right (I will go over this later on). You are usually paid as soon as the job is done and often in cash (although you have to record this and pay tax, also covered later on). There is always the possibility of expanding your business in a few year and taking on an employee, this will significantly increase your earnings if it is done correctly.

Now the negatives

1. Where is my next job coming from? - If you are self employed then you will always have this worry at the back of your mind, I still think it and it is always a possibility. It can be a real concern in the depths of winter but realistically for 10 months of the year there will always be work out there for good gardener.

- Injury or illness – There is no sick pay for a self employed gardener and if you are used to having a few dubious sick days in your current job then you will soon change when you don't get paid for them. There is also the sense that you are letting people down by not turning up and rather than phoning one boss, you may have to contact 5-6 different people to explain your absence. There are some insurance companies that can cover you for injuries and illness but these will be expensive and I personally do not use them but if you have financial commitments like a family and a mortgage then it is probably worth considering. You will have to look after your body, for example I used to play football with a fellow self employed gardener who played in goal. He broke his wrist one week and so couldn't work for a couple of months. If you have taken time to establish a good group of regular customers and then suddenly have to take time off then they might not wait for you.

- Taking the leap – If you are in a steady job with a guaranteed income then it can be a risk to suddenly give it all up for a career with no fixed income. If you have savings and no responsibilities then it is not so much of a problem but if you have a family to support then there is risk involved and you will most likely face a year at least of not earning as much as you would like. You should also consider that these days there is probably no such thing as a secure job.

- Start up costs – I will cover what you will need for start up later on but it must also be considered here. I already had a Citroen Picasso that I used, at the very least you will need an estate car or a van to fit all of your tools in. Then there is the cost of the tools, you can start off with borrowed or second hand but eventually, and as soon as you can, you will need to be getting quality professional and expensive tools to help justify charging higher prices. You will also find that in the long run, more expensive tools work out cheaper as they do a quicker job and last longer.

- Rain – If it is raining then there is not much that you can do. Mowing lawns is not really possible in heavy rain and power tools are not ideal. It is not worth sitting in the heavy rain and weeding a border as it will be far too unpleasant. I often find that even if I was willing to work through the rain then the customer will call to cancel anyway. Customers are generally very understanding about this but you will not get paid. I probably average about 10 days a year when I am rained off but I live in Bournemouth so this may be more of an issue in other parts of the country. Rainy or snowy days can be used in other ways such as maintaining tools, sorting your books, reading up on gardening or arranging your diary.

- Winter – In the depths of winter when you can't feel your fingers and toes then you may wonder why you ever chose to do this when you could be in a nice warm office. Just remember that it won't last and that they will be envious of you in the summer. Work does slow down as you get to the winter and you become limited to about 6 hours a day's work anyway due to the lack of daylight. I find that I will be busy right up until Christmas and then January and February are quieter. You can combat this by trying to find customers that will keep you on all year or just enjoying the time off as you prepare for the long busy summer ahead.

- Working alone – This might be a positive for you but for some it can be difficult. I can go a full day without speaking to anyone or just exchanging pleasantries with the customer before I start work. However, there are some customers that will work with you or come out and chat to you which can be nice.

Combine the above points with any other personal factors that you may have and see if you still want to be a professional gardener.

What services can I offer?

You will have to think about this before you start. I went straight into offering gardening services without any direct previous experience of gardening. I had previously worked for the countryside service of my local council so I had some knowledge of wild plants and knowledge of how to use all of the power tools required but this was about where my skills ended. I offered all aspects of gardening maintenance, on my website and leaflets I said lawns, hedges, weeding and small tree work.

If you are like me and had limited experience of gardening then it is probably worth doing some wider reading before you start and if you can, do a couple of practice sessions on friends' or relatives' gardens. Some companies will specialise in just doing lawns or just doing hedges and this can work well but bear in mind that you may be making your work even more seasonal by doing this.

You may be able to find a niche or a gap in the market that can give you a competitive edge and suit your particular skill set. For example, I started by offering wildlife friendly gardening as it matched my background and made me stand out from the crowd.

You will find that the learning curve is very steep. A lot of the customers have employed you because they are very keen gardeners and now can not keep up with the maintenance for health reasons. In this case they will often tell you exactly what they want you to do so gardening knowledge is not essential. These sorts of customers are very useful if you are just starting up as they can teach you a lot.

I am often asked if I can do hard landscaping and the temptation is to just say yes to every request when you have just started out. I now like to stick to jobs that I know I can do to a good standard so I don't quote for hard landscaping or fencing. If you are confident enough to take on a wide variety of jobs then do so, but don't feel like you have to. It is far better to do a good job of something that you are confident doing. You may also find that you get in over your head and start a job that you just don't have the experience or resources to finish to an acceptable standard.

A common job is weeding a border. I know of some gardeners that will refuse to do weeding but I don't really have a problem doing it. You will have to decide for yourself but you will be limiting the work that you can do if you decide not to weed. If it is a nice day and you have the radio on then I think it can be a nice way to spend an afternoon.

Some people will ask what qualifications you have and when you are new to the job it can be a bit awkward trying to explain that you actually don't have any gardening specific qualifications. I have probably only been asked this about 5 times in the last 3 years so it is unlikely to slow you down. If it does bother you then there are Royal Horticultural Society courses that you can take that can be done at distance. The total cost of course literature and exams is about £300. I took the RHS Level 2 Certificate in the Principles of Garden Planning, Establishment and Maintenance but found that most of what I was learning had very little relevance to the work that I was doing. However, it does look good to have on your website and to say to people when they ask. Alternatively, if you have the time and money to spare then there are many agricultural colleges across the country that offer longer horticultural courses.

It is also important to remember that there are some jobs that you can not do if you do not have the right qualifications. If you are going to be charging money for applying pesticides then you have to be qualified to do so. It is probably unlikely to be an issue if you are just using a spray that someone has given you and asked you to spray a few weeds on their driveway, although still technically illegal. You may find that you need to take the PA1 and PA6 courses in order to get any commercial work. I would also strongly advise against doing any chainsawing unless you have some qualifications. Apart from being extremely dangerous in the wrong hands, you will not be insured. Try to remember that landscape gardeners and tree surgeons are specialised professions and you are unlikely to be able to do the work that they do.

If you are worried that you do not have the skills required to be a gardener then I would tell you that it is unlikely to hold you back. So long as you are enthusiastic, friendly and polite then you will get on fine and will learn very quickly. For many customers, the fact that you are reliable and friendly will more thn compensate for any lack of gardening knowledge.

Getting started

So, you have read this far and are still keen on becoming a gardener? Good choice, I will now run through what you will need to do before you can start earning money.

Start up money can be a stumbling block for some people as you will need a significant amount to invest in tools. However, compared to most new businesses, the costs are relatively small.

Equipment

Vehicle

The first thing that you need to sort out is your transport. Some gardeners get by without a car or van and will use a bike or walk. This is possible in theory but does put a limit on the work that you can do. You will not be able to transport many tools around with you so this can limit the amount that you will be able to charge, but you can market yourself as an eco-gardener. If you are having to borrow the customer's lawn mower then I don't think that you can get away with charging as much as someone that brings their own professional equipment. It also will mean that your catchment area will be much smaller so it may take longer to establish a full diary. Another point to consider is that it will put a limit on the services that you can offer. For example, you will not be able to take waste away or bring in new plants, these can both be good ways to make extra money. There can be occasions where using a bike and trailer can be the best option. If you are just starting and working weekends or evenings then it can save a large initial outlay while you are making your mind up. If you live in a large city, particularly London, then it may be the best way to get around.

If you do decide to get a vehicle then you will need to think about what sort of services you will be offering. When I decided to start, I already had a large car that was able to fit all of the tools that I wanted. Luckily, I had passed my trailer licence a couple of years previously in an old job so I was able to put a tow bar on my car and get a cheap second hand trailer. You will need to read up on the DVLA website about the law on towing a trailer as it varies depending on your age and the weight of the trailer. The trailer was necessary for me because there are certain jobs that are just not possible with a car alone. If you are ever going to be taking on big jobs such as a very overgrown garden, then you will most likely be asked to remove the green waste. These jobs can be very profitable so the trailer soon pays for itself.

The main advantages of using a large car rather than a van is that there is a chance that you already have a suitable vehicle in your driveway. The vehicle will then double up as a family car at weekends and evenings and your business vehicle during the week. Bear in mind that once a family car becomes a work vehicle, it will be messy and have a spider web in every corner. You will probably not mind this but partners may not be so happy about it. A van can look more professional and you can put the name of your business and contact number on the side of it for advertising wherever you go. The time will probably come when you want to upgrade to a van, it did with me after about 3 years. I chose a Ford Transit as it was the right size for me. I think this type of van is best but others go for a flat bed tipper style van. These are far better for remving and disposing of waste but I have always thought it makes it difficult to keep your tools secure while on site as they cant all be locked away. For the rest of the book I will refer to using a car as this is how I started.

You will need to make sure that your vehicle is reliable and plan carefully when you get its MOT done. If your car doesn't start on a Monday in a busy spring then it can cost you a lot of money in lost work. People will be mostly understanding if you have car trouble once but if it happens more than that then they may start to look elsewhere. You will also start to create a back log of work that you may struggle to catch up with. Plan to get the car's MOT and service done in January or February when the work is slower and you will not miss so much work. I usually take a holiday in February so I leave the car in the garage while I am away so that no extra work is missed. In my second year of working, I put a Friday aside to get the car's MOT and service done, thinking that if something did go wrong then they would have the weekend to sort it out and I would be back on the road by Monday at the latest. It ended up failing the MOT and a new part was needed that took over a week to arrive. I postponed my Monday work but then realised that I was never going to be able to catch up on all of this work so was forced to hire a van for a week. This was a cost that would have been easily avoided if I had put it into the garage while I was on holiday two months earlier.

Remember that a work vehicle will be used far more than any car that you have owned in the past. I do over 10,000 miles a year now and probably start the engine 6 times a day on average. This means that things will go wrong more often than when you were using your car just for a commute to work and so will cost more to keep on the road.

Tools

This depends very much on your budget. I now have all of the tools that I will need and my total outlay was probably in the region of £2000.

It took me about a year before I decided what tools I needed. Some I take out with me every day, and some I leave in the garage and only bring out when I know I will need them.

The tools that I take out every day are:-

Small mower

Strimmer

Long handled hedge cutter

Long handled pruning saw

Leaf blower

Hedge cutter

Dutch hoe

Brush

Rake

Pick axe

Spade

Loppers

Bowsaw

Garden fork

Small hand fork and trowel

Lawn edger

Secateurs

Lawn edging scissors

Petrol can containing unleaded petrol for the mower

Petrol can containing mixed 2 stroke for the poser tools

Sprayer for pesticides

Empty bags for garden waste

Ground sheets for hedge cuttings

I started off using some power tools that my dad gave me that had been sitting in the garage for a few years. They were in various conditions but none of them lasted for very long. This was fine as it meant that I did not have to invest a lot of money straightaway in a venture that I was not 100% sure was going to work. After a few months, and when I realised that the business was going to work and some of the tools given to me had started to fail, I invested in some more expensive professional tools.

Most people will want you to cut their lawns. I have the smallest Honda Izy and it is just about light enough for me to comfortably lift in and out of my car. This must be considered before you buy a mower. If you can't lift the mower in and out of your car, and I suspect that I will stop doing this as I get older, then you can get a couple of planks of wood to keep in the car to use as ramps. Remember that during the summer, this mower will be used everyday so if you do get a cheap one from a supermarket then it may not be happy with this sort of work load. As mentioned above, I started out with some tools that were only ever designed for occasional domestic use and they did not make it through the first year so it is worth researching and spending more money here.

You should try and learn how to service your mower as it will save you a lot of money in the long run. There is not a lot to it and there are plenty of instructional videos on the internet. Make sure that you keep the blades sharp and the underside as clean as you can. If you are regularly maintaining a garden then a good lawn cut is often the job that gives the biggest impact.

One of the few transferable skills for me from my previous job was that I had been using Stihl power tools. This was an advantage because I knew what to buy and the basics of how they worked. Because of this I purchased a Stihl Kombi engine and the strimmer, pole saw and hedge cutter attachments. Buying detachable parts allowed me to save a lot of room in my car. It also works out a bit cheaper than buying all three separately. However, you are then reliant on one engine for 3 vital tools, so if it were to break for whatever reason then the consequences are greater. I solved this by getting a second engine unit as back up but this is quite expensive to do. If you have a van or the space then getting these sorts of units may not be the better option. Another useful aspect of the Kombi system is that you can also buy an extension pole for it that will give you an extra 1 metre reach with the pole saw and hedge trimmer. I purchased Stihl simply because it is what I had previous experience with but there are other professional brands such as Husqvarna or Echo that are equally as good.

I use a long reach hedge cutter and a normal hand held hedge cutter. For a while I just used the long reach for all hedge cutting and it does a good job but eventually I decided to buy a top of the range hedge trimmer as I found that I was cutting more and more hedges. It was quicker and gave a neater finish so I was happy with the decision. If you are just starting up and are short of funds then you could probably get away with just one hedge trimmer and perhaps invest in another one later on.

The final power tool that you will need is a leaf blower. They are very simple to use and can leave areas looking much neater than you could ever get them with a brush. Peoples opinions of leaf blowers can often be that you are just blowing debris around and once the wind blows after you have left then it will all be back again. I have not found this to be the case and once you get the hang of how to use one properly you will be able to round up all the debris into a pile very quickly and dispose of it properly.

Remember that these power tools will almost definitely be 2 stroke engines and so will need an additive for the petrol. Your lawn mower however will run on just unleaded so you will need 2 petrol cans with you, preferably different looking ones to avoid confusion.

Depending on your knowledge of these power tools, servicing them regularly is probably a good idea. When you do, get them done in the winter when they are being used less and the shop will not be as busy so can get it done quickly. The situation that you must avoid is that spring suddenly comes around and everyone wants their lawns cut at once and you come to use your mower after no use all winter and it doesn't start. You will be missing out on work at a crucial time of the year and the repair shop will be full of people in a similar situation so it may take time to get it back. If your tools are kept well then they should last you for years.

A further decision that you will need to make is whether to buy new or second hand. This will obviously be influenced by your budget but even so it is not a clear cut decision. I have purchased a couple of tools second hand with mixed experiences. The leaf blower that I bought was half the price of a brand new one and has been very reliable. The combi engine that I purchased was also half the price of a new one but broke within about 6 months and needed a lot of work on it so was probably not worth it. Since then I have decided to buy new, partly because I know that I have many years gardening ahead of me and I will get full use from them and partly because I know that I will have somewhere to take them back to if something goes wrong. You must also take into consideration that the make of tools that you buy are serviceable somewhere near to you. Some shops will specialise in Husqvarna or Stihl and if you do buy something cheap then many repair shops will not want to work on it as it is simply not worth it.

I would always go with petrol tools where possible rather than electric. The electric ones can be cheaper and need less maintenance but are generally not as good. They are also dangerous if you use them in the rain and you may not always have access to a power source. There are some good, professional tools that run from battery power and I am sure there will come a day soon when these will replace the petrol tools but at the moment the battery life is not quite long enough and they are expensive.

The rest of the tools in my car are all hand tools and will be much cheaper, but there is still a huge difference between cheap and poorly made ones and expensive and well made ones. For example, I purchased a £5 edging tool from my local garden centre and broke it very quickly. I thought that it was only £5 and I may have been expecting too much of it so I purchased another one. This also broke very quickly so I chose a different brand and spent £25. This is still going strong 3 years later. Having said this, I do have some very cheap tools in my garage that have lasted a long time and show no signs of wear. My advice would be that if it looks cheap and you think it might break quickly then it is not worth it. A good spade or a good fork can last you for your whole career so spending a bit extra now is definitely worth it in the long run.

There are many other things that you may need but will be used less frequently. You will have to decide from experience whether they are worth the investment. Here are a few items that I have but are not necessarily essential to running a gardening business.

Ladders

Scarifier

lawn fertiliser spreader

chainsaw

leaf rake

If you end up with something that you find you never use then you should sell it. It will be taking up valuable garage space and you will often be suprised by how much an old or broken tool can fetch.

Premises

As a one man operation you can easily run your business from home with a laptop and a good filing system. You will certainly need a garage or shed and if there is not one attached to your house then you will need to rent one. You will probably have some valuable tools to store and so a shed may noy be suitable, You are also likely to need far more room as tool maintenance must be done somewhere as well. I didn't have a garage when I started so I used my sister's empty garage. This worked well but was a 20 minute drive away so it was not ideal. She then moved so I had to rent one for a few months, this also worked fairly well and £60 a month was not too expensive, however, it didn't seem very secure and I was concerned that I had all of my expensive tools in a garage that was quite isolated. Eventually I moved to a new house that had a garage with it and this makes life so much easier. I appreciate that this may not always be possible for everyone but the advantages are huge, having somewhere that you can spend time maintaining your tools and knowing that they are safe is a big benefit. If you do need to rent a garage then the local papers and internet are the best places to start looking, or even better, ask a friend or relative who has a garage if you can borrow it for a while. You may eventually expand beyond a one man operation and then you will have no choice but to rent out a larger storage space.

Insurance

You must get insurance, any commercial work will require it and even domestic customers will sometimes want to check that you have it. It will rarely, if at all be needed, but you must have it in case something goes wrong.

I have personally never paid to insure my tools but it is worth considering as a theft from your van or car could cost you over £1000.

The cost for insuring a self emplyed gardener is fairly cheap but it is probably worth getting a high level of public liability.

Uniform

This one is up to you, I see a lot of gardeners that look very casual in jeans or shorts and a t shirt but this is not for me as I think it looks unprofessional. I think that smart trousers and a polo shirt are the best option. I even found a website that will print the name of my business onto a polo shirt, I think that it shows the customer that this is your job and that you are a professional and it is not just a hobby to earn a bit of extra cash.

Get trousers with knee pad pockets. I cannot emphasise enough how grateful you will be for knee pads, you will be spending a lot of time on your knees weeding so a bit of extra protection will help a lot.

Steel toe cap boots are also a necessity, they will save you from injury far more than you will realise.

If you don't already have them, then a good set of waterproofs is worth the investment. It will allow you to work in the rain so they will quickly pay for themselves. They are likely to get dirty and ripped so don't spend too much and don't wear your favourite coat.

Other items to buy

Soon after starting you will realise that there are many other small things that you will need to purchase. It may seem for the first year that there is always something new that you need, but with the majority of the purchases, they will last you for your whole career.

On the administration side of the business you will need to get some folders to keep receipts and contacts in. You will also need a way of providing customers with a receipt but this will be covered further later on in the book.

Get yourself a diary with at least an A5 page per day and use it. Don't ever be tempted to think that you will remember something or that you know what you have to do today as it is easy for something to have slipped your mind and you will soon get unhappy customers.

I started off with a dedicated mobile phone for business use only but later found that I could save £10 a month by just using the same one for business and personal use. I would reccomend getting a landline as it can make you appear as a more established business.

I purchased some professional looking stationery. Some headed paper for quotes and some smart looking receipt books.

Naming your business can be tricky. It is worth spending some time thinking about it as it might be difficult to change in the future. If you are a sole trader then you don't have to worry too much about picking a unique name, I called myself 'Simon's Garden Services' as I thought it was simple and easy to remember but you can go for something more creative.

When To Start

This might not be your choice to make as people's circumstances are different. If you start in early January then you may be disheartened by how slowly you acquire customers. I started in March. This was not really my choice as it was when my previous job ended but it did happen to be a good time to start up. Now that I am established, I know that the first sunny weekend in March means that my phone is going to go mad and I will be working very long hours for the next few months. If you are in a steady job but are going to be gardening as a career change then I would aim to start at the beginning of March. If it is not your choice and you are starting up at any other time of the year due to circumstances beyond your control, then don't worry as with the right advertising there is always work to do.

Customers

Getting Customers

Unless you have a very large network of friends and family that all need gardening doing, you will need to invest in advertising. This can take many different forms and I have tried most of them with varying success.

Free advertising

There are many websites that will list businesses free of charge so it is worth spending an afternoon to register your gardening business with these, some examples include yell.com and freeindex but a simple search on Google will uncover many more and you have nothing to lose by registering with them.

Register you business with Google maps. This will mean that whenever anyone looks at your area on Google maps, then your business will appear. It also means that you are likely to get customers that are local to you.

Gumtree has been a good source of work for me, a simple advert on there will almost always give you a response, however they have started harging for business adverts now,

Word of mouth is probably the best way of getting new work that there is. People often ask friends if they know of a good gardener so make sure that all of your friends and family are aware that you are starting up and maybe even give them a few business cards. When you become more established, word of mouth will probably become all of the advertising that you need.

You can try approaching estate agents and property management companies but they are less likely to want to employ a new starter so this may be a good approach a couple of years down the line.

I have never been keen on going door to door. Some of my customers have told me that they have had people cold calling and saying things like "I notice that your hedge needs cutting, would you like a free quote." If you want to do this then it is up to you but I don't like the hard sell and prefer to put my advertising out and let the customer contact me.

My job beforehand was working on nature reserves so I had decided that my particular niche was going to be gardening with wildlife in mind. I contacted my local paper and said that I was starting my own wildlife friendly gardening business and asked if they would like to do an article on me. I was very surprised when they said yes and a few weeks later there was a full page article about my new business. This was a great boost in the early days and I would recommend trying it. There are probably all sorts of ways that you could make it newsworthy such as being made redundant and going it alone, if you are going to be extra environmentally conscious or even if it is just a standard new start up then it is worth sending them an email.

Cheap advertising

Get yourself some business cards printed and carry them with you all the time. While working, passers by or neighbours will often ask if you have a card that they could have. This will not always come to anything but is worth doing.

When I first started, I cycled to about 10 different newsagents and put a card in each of their windows. I got very few customers from this and have not done it since as it didn't seem worth the cost and effort. However, it is cheap and may work differently in your area. The main advantage is that you can target a specific area, either local to you, an area with lots of big gardens or an area with a high elderly population.

More expensive

A sign on your van with your name and phone number can be an excellent way of letting a lot of people know that you are a gardener. If it is parked in your drive every night then the whole of your street will instantly know that they have a local gardener. If you are parked at a customer's address all day or are there every week at the same time then people will notice. Alternatively, you could get a board to put out every time you stop to do work or leave one outside your house, this should have the same effect if you are working from a car instead.

An advert in the local paper is now the only advertising that I will invest money in. When I first started I took out 10 weeks of adverts.It was only 3 lines at the end of the paper but it worked well and got me most of my regular customers. The free paper goes to every single house in the town so I can think of no other advertising that is going to reach that many people. It is however, quite expensive and may cover an area that is too far away from you so don't be afraid to turn down a small mowing job on the other side of town. My add simply read, "Simon's garden services, lawns, hedges and small tree work, call for a free quote" and then include a phone number obviously. If you can, include a land line number as it can give a more professional appearance and can make you seem like more of an established business. My landline answer phone message then gives my mobile number in case someone wants an immediate response.

I have also tried an advert in a local free magazine. This was a half page of an A5 book that was delivered to houses in a particular region and has the advantage of being glossy and in colour so you can be a bit creative with your advert. I found this form of advertising to be a little expensive for the amount of leads that it provided for me. To reduce the price of your advert then you could try submitting an editorial to go alongside your advert. For example, I submitted a wildlife gardening article that was published with my advert. This gave me a slight reduction in cost and also provided me with lot more space.

Building a website can give you a chance to go into far more detail about you and the services that you offer. You can make many different pages that can highlight the services that you offer, some examples of you previous work and maybe some articles or gardening tips. This may not be for everyone as it can be expensive to keep it online and if you do not have the skills to maintain it then you will also have to pay for someone to do this.

Leaflets can be printed up fairly cheaply if you shop around and can give you a good amount of room to sell yourself. They can be delivered by employing a company to do it or you can just do it yourself and target specific areas

The type of advertising that you will do will be dependent on your start up budget. You will probably reach a point after a couple of years where you will only need the free forms of advertising like website listings, gumtree and most importantly, word of mouth to keep you in work.

Your advert should include a company name and a phone number, preferably a land line and a mobile. If there is room then the types of services that you are offering and an email or website address. You are always going to be expected to offer free quotes so you could include this on any advertising. You will not get very far by charging people for giving them quotes so you must include this time and travel in any pricing.

I don't think that it is advisable to include prices in your advert. My advert in the paper went alongside one that was offering gardening services "from £6 per hour" I am not quite sure how they managed to do this but it didn't seem to make any difference and people still called me. When someone phones me to enquire then I do not generally mention prices unless specifically asked as I like to see the garden and make a judgment based on that rather than guess over the phone.

One word of warning about advertising, if someone phones you to offer adverts then it is generally a good idea to politely decline. As soon as you register as self employed and start getting your adverts out, people will find you and try to sell you advertising space. I have had a couple of people call me and try and sell space in a charity magazine that they say is distributed in my local area. When I read up on them on the internet and in forums, it turns out that they are not always what they seem and are not worth the money. One person phoned me saying that last year I had promised to sponsor this charity magazine and he was calling to collect the money, I had only been in business for 3 weeks so had obviously made no such promise.

When Customers Phone

If you have done your advertising well then you will soon be receiving phone calls asking for quotes. If you can not answer the phone during the day, and very often you will not as you should be working, then I always try and return the call on the same evening. Sometimes this is not quick enough and they have found someone else but there is little that you can do about this.

The conversation will usually go along the lines of them asking you if you do hedges or if you do weeding and then I try and arrange a time to visit them and discuss the work that needs doing and the price. The end of the day is usually the best time as you never quite know how long you are going to be there. Some people will want a long discussion and will give you a long tour of their garden and a cup of tea. Others will just say that they want their lawn cutting and how much will it be.

The work that I do is either a set job that requires a set price e.g. cut the lawn for £25, or a general tidy up or maintenance that will require an hourly rate. If the job is continuous or has no definite end then I find that an hourly rate is far easier and will avoid any disagreements at the end. For example, if someone asks you to give their garden "a good tidy" then I would find it difficult to put a set price on this as people's interpretation of a good tidy can be very different. Instead, I will give them an hourly rate and estimate how long I think it will take me to get the garden into a good state. This avoids any disagreements at the end when you say that you are finished and the customer says that they expected more to be done. In this instance, if you had given a set price then doing more work would have to be at your cost but at an hourly rate then you will be able to charge more. In reality most people are very nice and this will rarely happen.

When going to give a quote it is very important to be there when you say you will. If I am going to be giving a quote at 5.30 then I will always say about 5.30 or say 5.30 to 6 as you will never know if your previous job will over run. If you end up running very late then make sure that you give them a call as soon as you can to let them know. People generally won't mind at all, so long as you tell them and apologise.

You will almost always be dressed in your gardening gear when you give a quote so try and make your clothes as smart as you can and dust your self down. You are a gardener so they should expect you to be a little bit muddy. Go in armed with your diary, a pen and a business card and be as polite and friendly as possible. Your first few quotes can be quite nerve racking and it is always tempting to give a very low price to make sure that you get the work. Try and avoid this as you will regret it as soon as you get the job. I have found that most people will not be shopping around and you are the only person that will be giving them a quote that day so as long as you don't give them a ridiculous price, then they will probably hire you.

When I first started, I found that a lot of my customers knew more about gardening than I did, and some still do. They are usually hiring a gardener because they have previously loved gardening themselves but are now unable to do it due to health or time restraints. So, you may be working for someone that has been working in that garden for over 30 years and will list off lots of Latin names of odd plants that you have never heard of. I have found that it rarely matters to the customer if you don't know the names of some plants, they just want someone enthusiastic and friendly. In these instances they will often give you very specific instructions every time anyway. Some will ask you the name of a plant, I find that most are simply interested in finding out more but I have had a couple that I got the feeling that they were testing my knowledge.

Keeping Customers

Gardening is different to many trades in that you can keep returning to the same customers over and over again. A job that is done one year, will usually need doing again the following year so if they like you then you will have a job for the forseeable future. For this reason it is very important that the customer is happy with the work that you do as word will spread and you will save a lot of money on advertising.

It is very important to arrive when you say you will. Punctuality is almost as important as the work that you do and when I first started I was surprised that people were so pleased that I simply arrived on time and consistently when I said I would. This should not be hard to achieve if you keep your diary well organised. The nature of the job means that it can be difficult to know when you will finish somewhere and so you may be forced into running late but so long as you let your customers know as soon as you can that this will be the case then they will rarely mind.

I try and keep communication levels high between my customers and myself. This is particularly important for customers that are not in when I do my work. You will find that this will happen a lot as they will be out at work when you need to come. They will usually leave your money in a safe place along with some instructions or if it is a regular customer then I often try to give them my bank details and then invoice them at the end of the month.

I have some customers that i have had for a few years now, but only seen face to face on a handful of occasions. In these instances I like to get an email address so that I can explain the work that I have done that day and ask about future work.

When Things Go Wrong

This is not really something that you will want to think about but, occasionally, things may go wrong. For example, in my first couple of years I cut a phone line with a hedge cutter, smashed a conservatory window when I caught a stone with my strimmer and popped a tyre on a customers mini tractor that I was driving. In all these cases the customer was very understanding and apart from me having to cover the costs incurred, there was no harm done and all continued to be regular customers. Most people will understand that mistakes happen and so long as you are honest about what happened and are willing to cover the costs then there should be no problem. You will have insurance to cover anything major that might happen or the customer might have home insurance that could help you out.

No matter how good you are, you will inevitably receive the occasional complaint. Gardening tasks can be subjective and your idea of a good hedge cut might be different from the customers. If you are charging an hourly rate then it will not be such a problem but if you quoted for the job and end up having to do it twice then you will end up loosing money. You can reduce the chances of this happening by being as clear as you can when discussing the quote and be as specific as possible about the details. Almost all of the time, the best way to handle the situation is to just go back and do the work again as this will avoid any bad publicity for you and the stress of having an unhappy customer. You will probably start to get a sense of whether people are likely to be awkward customers when you first meet them and the longer you work, the more you will find yourself dealing with people that you have worked for before so situations like this should become less and less.

Making Money

You will no doubt have a love for gardening and will hopefully enjoy your time being self employed, however, you need to make money and make sure that you make enough money to cover all of your costs and have enough left over to make a good living wage.

When people are starting up, the first thing they want to know is how much to charge. This is a very difficult question to answer as prices vary depending on a number of factors. I can tell you that in 2020, the going rate in my area of Bournemouth is about £20 per hour but this does not tell the whole story and you will need to do some research yourself to figure out your pricing methods. Prices can change in different areas of the country, what specific job you are doing and the tools that you use. For example, if you are in London or the Southeast of the country and turn up in a nice new van with lots of expensive power tools then your hourly rate would be much different than someone in the north of the country that turns up on a bike and uses the customer's hand tools. You will need to do some calculations for yourself and work out all of your overheads. This will include the cost of buying, maintaining and running of all of your toolsand you will end up driving a lot of miles so also include the cost of maintaining your car, petrol and travel time. Then you must decide how much money you need to have coming in. Don't sell yourself short here, a good gardener is in high demand and you should be paid accordingly.

When I started, I asked a friend who was already a gardener, what he was charging and also emailed a couple of local gardeners who were good enough to respond. This gave me a rough idea of what I could reasonably charge when I was doing my first quotes. You will soon get an idea for yourself about pricing once you have done a few quotes. While it can be difficult to take rejection by a customer that says you are charging too much, you equally do not want to be in a situation where all of your quotes are being accepted as this will most likely mean that you are not charging enough.

I was more comfortable charging an hourly rate at first as I did not really have a good idea how long it would take me to do some jobs and an hourly rate can give you some security and allow you to manage your diary much easier. However, if someone asks you to do a specific job such as mow my lawn or cut my hedge, then an hourly rate is not really appropriate and the customer just wants a price. I usually try and imagine how long it will take me to do the job and relate the price that I give to my hourly rate but usually make it more. For example, if I was asked to cut a lawn and I estimate that it will take me 30 minutes to do it, I will probably quote somewhere between £20-25 if my usual hourly rate is £20.

I now prefer to give prices for completing the job rather than working by the hour as I have found that I can make much more money this way. You are incentivised to work faster and also to invest in good tools. For jobs like hedge cutting, pesticide spraying and anything involving a chainsaw, you will be able to charge a lot more than a standard hourly rate. I also have some jobs, particularly blocks of flats, where I give a set price per visit on the condition that I keep them looking well maintained. This means that I can earn a lot more and in the future it may be easier to take on an employee with this pricing structure.

You should think about having a minimum price. Someone may want a very small patch of grass cut regularly that may only take you 5 minutes but If you charge in the same was as you would a larger lawn then it may not be worth your while. You will have to consider travel time and probably charge no less than your standard hourly rate, even if it does only take you 5 minutes.

Some customers will try and negotiate with you when you are quoting but I have never entered into this as I feel like it cheapens the service that you offer. I will offer the price that I am willing to do it for and not change it. If they want to reduce the amount that you do for a cheaper price then that is fine but don't let them talk you into a lower price, especially if they say "is there a reduction for cash in hand"

As you progress in your gardening career, you will take some customers with you and will probably be their gardener for many years and in some cases become friends. This brings with it the tricky subject of price increases. I have done quotes for people that are replacing their current gardener due to retirement and are shocked by my price. I can only assume that this is because their current gardener has not bothered to increase his prices and so is working for a rate that he set 30 years ago. Jobs for property management companies are easy as they will understand an annual increase due to inflation and you wont feel quite so embarrassed asking a company for more money as you will an old lady. There is no easy way to do this but you must do it. I would recommend a small increase every 2-3 years and explain fully why you are doing this. If it is just a couple of pounds then they will almost always understand and be happy to pay the extra. If you keep avoiding the issue then your pay in real terms will continue to fall every year.

A good time to do it would be either at the start of the calendar year, straight after your Christmas break or at the start of the financial year in April. If you are confident that you can keep track of what prices you charge to different people then it may be easier to test the water with a higher rate for new customers before you ask existing customers for a rise. This will show you that there are people willing to pay your new prices.

Extras

Make sure that you charge for anything extra that you do that was not included in the original quote. Most people will offer this up front but some will try to take advantage. If you have quoted to cut a hedge and someone then asks "could you just trim this shrub at the front while you are here" then you must add some onto the original price as it is only fair. You are running a business and should not be expected to do things for free. When quoting, you should also get into the habit of asking what they want to be done with the green waste. Many people have green bins, compost sites or fire sites that will take all of the waste but if they want you to take it away and dispose of it then make sure that you consider this in your prices. You may automatically include taking the waste away in your price and this is fine but be sure not to do a job and then find that once you have paid to get rid of the green waste, you have barely made any money.

If you are asked to provide and use some pesticide then add on a few pounds for this. I purchased a 5 litre bottle of concentrated round up when I started and am gradually working my way through it. Whenever I use it I add on at least a couple of pounds to the price, even though I probably only use about 10 pence worth. The same can be said of buying plants or other materials such as bark or compost for a customer. Make sure that you don't just charge what you paid for them, you should consider the time that it has taken you to get these products and transport them. You should also check at any garden centre or DIY store for a trade discount as this could potentially increase your profit margin still further.

I don't like to be pushy when it comes to selling these extras but there are some things that can be gently suggested that can make you extra money. A good example is a lawn treatment in the spring and autumn. You can buy the fertiliser in bulk and then charge a bit extra for applying it. If you have the space then you could try growing your own plants to sell to the customers.

These 'extra' charges will apply mostly to when you are maintaining someone's garden and charging an hourly rate, otherwise they should already be included in your price.

Who to work for?

You will find that some people are far better to work for than others. You should consider if you like working at a specific location primarily but you should also consider how profitable the job is. Financial factors to be considered should be

How long does it take to get there?

How much work is there to do?

Do they tip well?

Do they pay on time?

Do they often cancel at the last minute?

Are they flexible with the time and day?

Can you go early?

Travel time should always be considered in your quote. If it takes 30 minutes to drive to a garden and then 30 minutes to get back then there is an extra hour of lost time. If it is just to do a small lawn then chances are that it is not going to be worth it. If you are traveling for 30 minutes and there is a full day's work, then it probably will be worth it.

Some people will tip if they like you and you do a good job, this can be a factor in deciding if you want to keep a customer as it can be a significant boost to your earnings.

Most domestic customers will pay you as soon as the job is done but if you start working for property management companies or blocks of flats then the payment can be some time in coming. You must take into account the amount of time that it will take you to send invoices and to keep track of who has paid you. If someone regularly takes 3 months and 5 reminders to pay, then it is probably time to let them go. I have had the occasional customer that has been 50 pence short when it comes to payment, I let it go but I usually find that I don't work for them much longer If you do the work then you deserve to be paid the full amount on time and you should not accept anything less.

Some customers can be prone to cancelling at short notice. If they do this regularly then you should not work for them for much longer. I very often have a very full diary and if someone cancels on me at the last minute then I can probably go to a different job to fill the time, but not always. They will be costing you money in wasted time so don't stand for it. If it is pouring down with rain and they are not sure that there is much that you can do then this is a different matter and you should probably try and leave a little bit of time free in your diary in case this happens

When you start to get a full diary then you will realise that a customer that says "just come whenever you can" is very valuable to you. They make it much easier to organise your diary and means that if bad weather hits or someone cancels last minute, then you can quickly change your day. Blocks of flats and commercial contracts are probably most likely to be like this.

As your diary gets full, you will probably want to start earlier and earlier so finding people that are ok with you starting at 8am can be very useful.

It is a good idea to keep more than one copy of all of the contact addresses and numbers. You may be able to remember most of the addresses as you will be visiting them regularly or have them written in your diary but you won't know the phone numbers and if you lose your mobile phone then you will be in trouble. Keep a file with all addresses and phone numbers of anyone that you have worked for as you never know when you might need it.

Where to Work

The closer the jobs are to your house or garage, the better. When you are driving to a new job, you are not earning any money so you need to aim to keep it to a minimum. The distance you drive to a job needs to be proportional to how much money that you will be able to make there. If you drive 30 minutes for a 15 minute lawn cut then it is not going to be worth it but if you can stay working at the one place or in that local area all day then it probably will be worth it. You need to group jobs as best you can. This can be difficult as some people may not be available on certain days or some people prefer mornings or some prefer a Thursday or Friday so that they can enjoy the garden more at weekends. This is another reason why customers that are flexible with times are very valuable to you. I have a look at my diary each winter and see if I can move some regular jobs around to make less driving time and I almost always can.

Common Jobs

I will not be able to teach you how to garden in this book but I can give you some pointers and advice that would have helped me in the early days. One of my main worries was that I would just get to the job and not know what I was doing, in reality this never happened. Most customers will give you specific instructions but there are a few basics that you should know.

Weeding

Weeds can be a misleading term as it is essentially the wrong plant in the wrong place. Not everyone has the same idea of what a weed is and people often ask me if a certain plant is a weed. I will usually know exactly what this plant is but the question of whether it is a weed or not is not clear cut.

Some people may say to you "just pull out the weeds" or "you know which ones the weeds are don't you". There are some obvious weeds that it is very unlikely that anyone will ever want growing in their garden. I would recommend looking at pictures of the following so that you know what they look like.

Bindweed

Bramble

Chickweed

Goose grass

Couch grass

Dandelion

Dock

Enchanters nightshade

Ground elder

Groundsel

Hairy bittercress

Sycamore seedlings

Nipplewort

Petty surge

Plantain

Stinging nettles

I have never come across anyone that wanted to keep any of the plants in the above list so you should be safe removing them from anywhere in the garden.

There are some plants that can fall on either side of the weed line and here you will have to make a judgment on the type of garden or just ask the owner.

Aquilegia – has a very nice flower but can spread quickly so not everyone will like it

Bluebells – Most of the bluebells that you will find in gardens will be Spanish bluebells and be much larger and more invasive than the native variety. I would always ask the customer before removing them as most people really like them, however, they do spread very fast and could take over the garden if not kept in check

Buddleia – Many people have a buddleia in their garden and garden centres will sell them. They also self seed very readily and will crop up in all sorts of places, usually the seedlings should be removed

Campanula - This plant can provide good ground cover and has some nice flowers but it does spread very rapidly and should probably be kept under control, if not removed

Celandine – These are a very attractive yellow flower in early spring. The bulbs are difficult to remove and will form a thick carpet of foliage if left uncontrolled.

Buttercups – They should usually be removed but occasionally people will want them in the garden

Feverfew – I almost always leave this as it is a nice white flower, but some will not want it

Forget-me-not – A lovely carpet of small blue flowers can be formed but they will spread quite quickly if not controlled

Foxgloves – They form a very large and attractive flower that are great for wildlife so unless told otherwise, I leave them. They will take 2 years to flower so it will look like there are weeds in the borders for the first year as it will just be leaves.

Green alknet – Despite the name they have a blue flower, I usually remove them as they can dominate other plants but others may like them

Herb Robert – Almost always removed but a good wildflower for insects

Honesty – A nice purple flower in the spring but can spread quickly if it is not controlled

Pendulous sedge – I will always remove new seedlings and often the seed heads from established plants to try and stop them spreading. It can add a nice foliage to a garden but no flowers

Poppy – They are often classed as weeds but I would never remove them unless told specifically to do so as they are a very attractive plant

Ragwort – Almost always remove but as with Herb Robert, they are good for wildlife

Rosebay willowherb – They are a nice tall pink flower but usually removed as they spread very quickly

Teasel – The foliage can look unsightly in a flower bed so they will usually be removed but the flower head is quite unique and good for wildlife

Thistle – Almost always considered a weed to be removed but when in flower, can look good

Violet – They can provide good ground cover and an attractive small flower but will continue to spread

Strawberry – unless the area of the garden is being specifically used to grow strawberries then they should be removed as they are very vigorous and will spread quickly.

The general theme with the above plants is that they can be attractive but will spread quickly if left unmanaged. You can make a judgment call on the style of the garden, for example, if it is a cottage garden with very full borders and little soil on show then many of the above plants can be left in but if it is a very formal garden with neat borders and shrubs then they will almost all need to be removed. If in doubt then ask the customer and explain the value of leaving them and of removing them.

Once you have weeded a few borders, you will soon know all of the plants listed here.

In the early stages of your life as a gardener, you will probably find it difficult to say no to jobs but as you build up a good customer base and can afford to be a little more picky with jobs then the weeding jobs will probably be the first to go. It can be nice on a decent day to work your way through a border with your radio on to keep you company but too much of it will probably take its toll mentally and physically. Also, you must bear in mind that weeding is very time consuming and if you spend a couple of hours weeding then you may only manage to do a few metres of flower bed. If you had spent the same two hours cutting hedges and mowing a lawn then the results are far more impressive and so you can probably charge more.

Once you have mastered identifying the weeds, there are a few shrubs and flowers that you should also make sure that you can recognise. It may seem like there are an endless number of different plants to learn but once you have visited a few gardens you will start to realise that there are a few plants that are very popular and you will be dealing with a lot.

Camellia – They have wonderful large flowers for about a month in early spring. The reason that you need to know about them is that they usually don't need to be cut as it will affect the next years flowering. If you do need to trim them then it should only be just after they have finished flowering, otherwise, they will have very few flowers in the next year.

Clematis – These can be tricky to deal with but many people have them because they have such large and colourful flowers. They are a climber that will often need to be guided but the real challenge comes after this. Some species require a hard cut back i.e. almost right to the ground and some need just a trim of the dead material. Another thing to be careful of, and a good reason why you should familiarise yourself with them as soon as you can, is that in the winter they look very much like they have died and can quite easily be mistaken for a herbaceous perennial and pulled out.

Laurel – There is not a lot that you need to know about laurel as it is a very robust plant and can generally be pruned whenever it needs it but you should know what it looks like as you will come across it in a lot of gardens as it is a very popular hedging plant.

Wisteria – A popular climber that looks very nice when flowering in spring but they require some quite precise cutting back. They are cut twice a year, once around July and once around February. The summer cut should be to cut the new shoots back to about 5-6 leaves. In the winter, cut the same growth to 2-3 leaves to keep it under control.

Fruit trees – All a bit different but if you are asked to cut one back and the customer does not know how then you need to do a bit of research as a false move could mean no fruit for the following year. For example, apple trees come in 2 types, tip barers and spur barers and so you will need to know the variety to be sure of fruit the following year.

Rose – Many gardeners think that pruning a rose is difficult but it really is not. Cut out any dead or obviously diseased stems. With the exception of climbing roses, a rose should be cut back in late winter, usually low to encourage vigorous growth. They are dead headed regularly throughout the summer and respond very well to feeding. They are also prone to aphid and fungus attacks so a regular spray will benefit them.

Leylandii – Very common hedge or standard plant and are generally liked because they are evergreen and very fast growing. They can look very neat when they are cut well but the main thing to be careful of is to not cut past the green. If you cut a branch back too far then it will never grow again so unlike most other hedges, if you gave it a very hard cut back then you will kill it and it wont recover. So, always leave it green when you have cut it.

This list is by no means exhaustive but you really need to know a bit about them as you will definitely have to deal with them at some point. It may also be worth visiting a gardn centre and having a look at these plants rather than just relying on a picture.

Lawns

From March to October, mowing can make up a lot of your work day. I have some customers that will do their own lawn and just need me to do other tasks but these are the exception. If a customer just wants their lawn mowing then I will usually just give a set price depending on the size of the lawn and the frequency. Some people will want it cutting once a week as they will want it looking good all the time, others once every fortnight, every 3 weeks or every month so make sure that you take this into account when you are giving your quote. If a lawn is going to be cut once a week then then it will be a much shorter visit than if it is cut once a month, so price accordingly.

You must also take into account the type of lawn that you are going to be cutting. Some people take great pride in their lawns and will have a company like Greenthumbs in to care for it regularly, these people are also likely to want a cut once a week. Others will just want it cut when it starts to look untidy, these will probably want once every 3-4 weeks and are likely to be full of moss and weeds. The difference in these types of lawns, as you will find out, is that they can take different amount of times to cut. A lawn that is weed and moss free and made up of thick grass will take longer to cut and will test your mower, if the blades are blunt then it will show and you will struggle. A lawn that is moss and weeds is usually much easier to cut, so long as you are cutting above the level of the moss.

I have not got a mower with a roller and have never had a customer that was concerned by this. A roller will give a more professional and neat finish and will mean that you have to do stripes in the lawn otherwise it will look terribly messy.

You will usually be expected to do the edges as well, this can be done with a strimmer or edging shears. If there is a defined edge between he lawn and beds then the edging shears are probably the best option as it will leave a much neater finish. If it is a less formal lawn and it goes right up against the fence, a building or there are trees in the middle of it then a strimmer will be needed. I strim and cut edges before mowing as the mower can then pick up more of the grass but you can do it the other way around. When strimming, be very careful of stones and pay attention to which way the head is turning. Make sure that you are not likely to flick a stone towards any windows or cars as this will cost you.

Mowing is the task that is most affected by rain. If it is raining then you can do some tasks such as hedge cutting or weeding but not lawn cutting. It is even difficult if it has rained earlier in the day but if you choose the right mower then it can be done. The main problem is that your mower will not pick up the grass very well and you will find that you leave large lumps of grass behind you.It can also mean that the grass will lie flat and so not reach the blades. If you have a mower with a roller then the pick up of wet grass is generally not very good. Makes such as Honda or Etesia are considered good models for wet weather mowing. Often the customer will call you and cancel anyway if it is raining. If you keep your mower clean, particularly the bag, then mowing can be done in the wet and give good results. It can help to do it on a slightly higher setting or even go over it twice to pick up any grass that was not done the first time. Equally if there has been an extremely dry spell then firstly, lawns may not grow much due to lack of water and secondly your mower will kick up a lot of dust. In this case you must keep the mower's air filter clear.

Watch out for hazards in the lawn. Most customers with dogs will pick up any mess before you arrive but it is not a good idea to just mow over it if they do not. Try and avoid taking on lawns that are full of stones as this can do some severe damage to your mower and if you are particularly unlucky then the mower might kick one up and throw it into a conservatory window.

When performing the first cut of the year then it is common practice to leave it a bit higher than you normally would as it can damage the grass taking it down low. It can then be gradually lowered. You will find that people like it done at very different lengths and some will want it as low as you can possibly get it, you should consider this when you are providing a quote. The last cut of the year should also be slightly higher than you have been doing during the summer.

Hedge cutting

Along with a good mower, a good hedge cutter is the most important item that you will buy. Make sure that you can easily lift it and that it is a good make. I have found that of all gardening jobs that I quote for, hedge cutting can make the most money as it is a job that many people can struggle with and the results are instant and impressive. If you have a good hedge cutter then an overgrown hedge can be cut back in no time at all while the customer may have been trying to do it with shears or a cheap electric cutter. The top of the hedge can take more time if you can not reach it with your regular cutter. Ladders or/and a long handled cutter may be needed and this will take a bit longer but if you are using ladders and a long handled hedge trimmer then it is unlikely that the customer would stand a chance of being able to do it themselves and so your services are more valuable.

Weeding, lawn cutting and hedge cutting are going to be your most common requests and you should concentrate on mastering these tasks. There are many other straight forward tasks that you will be asked to do at some point such as planting, digging up a shrub, weed spraying and leaf clearing. There are also more specialist tasks that you may be asked to do such as fencing or laying a new lawn but this is up to you and whether you feel confident enough to take them on. Don't be afraid to say no to jobs that you are not comfortable with, you will probably regret taking it on and waste yours and your customer's time and money.

When on a job, I often try to consider who I am working for and tailor the work that I do to meet their needs. For example, looking after the grounds of a block of flats will require different work to an old lady's small and pristine garden. A block of flats will usually require a quick tidy, hedge cut and lawn cut, any overgrown areas or beds could be strimmed or hoed or sprayed but a smaller domestic garden may need everything to be perfect and weeding and edging of the lawn is required. This is a very crude example and will not always apply but hopefully give you an idea of how the way you work needs to be adapted to the customer.

Health and safety

When you are self employed, if you get injured or are ill then no one will pay you so you must look after yourself. I would never do a job without steel toe cap boots on as it is far too easy to drop something on your toes, you will probably not realise this until you are doing some gardening and not wearing them.

I see a lot of gardeners working without ear protection and if you are just mowing your own lawn once in a while then it is not a problem but when it is your job and you are spending most of every day with these noisy machines then it will start to take its toll in later life if you do not take precautions.

Strimming and hedge cutting will also require some form of face and eye protection. I use a helmet with ear defenders and a visor attached but safety glasses could do the job as well.

You will find that you get through gloves at an alarming rate. I would recommend wearing them as much as you can, partly for safety as you never quite know what is going to be in the soil that you plunge your hands into and partly as if you do not then your hands will start to become a mess with cuts and calluses very quickly.

Buy yourself some trousers with knee pad pockets or get some attachable knee pads. You spend a lot of time on your knees clearing various debris from the ground so knee pads are very useful.

Vibration white finger is a hazard of the job and should be taken very seriously. It is a condition that is caused by using high vibration power tools regularly and can cause you a lot of pain in later life. The ways to avoid this are to use tools with a lower vibration, usually the more expensive ones, and to take regular breaks if you need to be using them all day. There are some gloves on the market that claim to reduce the vibrations but there is some debate as to whether they are effective. Having cold hands can also make you more susceptible so wearing gloves in this instance would be very beneficial.

Being a gardener and suffering from hayfever is a very bad combination but it can be managed. You could start taking the tablets early on in the season to build your resistance. I personally suffer when cutting lawns which is obviously not ideal but I have overcome this by wearing a ventilator mask. It looks a little excessive but does the job well.

Depending on your complexion, you may well get through a lot of suncream in a good summer. You are going to be out in the sun a lot so it is important to keep reapplying with a high factor and to keep well hydrated. Consider buying a coolbox for your lunch and drinks. A sun hat is also a good purchace for the very hot days.

If you end up doing some commercial work then some companies will require you to fill out a risk assessment or send them your health and safety policy. They can just send you a from to fill in that will generally be straight forward but if they just ask you to send them your health and safety policy then it is usually easy enough to find a template on the internet.

Other things to consider

Eventually you may want to buy yourself a small radio to keep you company on the long days of weeding borders. It can make the days go much faster and is a much more practical alternative to wearing headphones.

You may not consider this when you first start but toilet breaks can be an issue on certain jobs.Don't be tempted to go in a customers garden as it is extremely unprofessional and if you are caught then you will almost certainly loose a customer. Don't be afraid to ask the customer to use their toilet. If you are doing jobs that last for 2 hours or more then it is reasonable for the customer to expect you to need the toilet, especially after all the cups of tea that they will be giving you. You will end up with some customers that are not in when you visit so in this instance it is good to know where all the local public toilets or larger supermarkets are.

Throughout the year

Jobs change as the year goes on and you will find that certain times of the year are far busier than others. This is the nature of the job and you will probably have to work more in the spring and summer than you will in the winter.

January to February

This is the quietest time of the year and the time that you should get some other things done. I get my cars MOT done, go on holiday, give my tools a good service, tidy the garage, do the taxes and generally prepare for the upcoming busy season.

There will be work for you to do but there will be more rainy days and maybe even snowy days when you will not be able to get things done. If the weather is mild and you have some regular customers that want to keep you on during the winter then there will be work to do. It will mostly be tidying or preparation work such as building a compost bin, turning the compost, spreading mulch around re-establishing edges to the beds or fencing.

You will find that you are limited by the hours of daylight anyway as it is dark by 4pm so I often just accept that I will not be getting too much work done at this time of year and take it easy because as soon as the weather changes you will be working hard.

March – April

There will be one sunny weekend in March when people will realise that they would like there garden to be in good shape for the up coming summer and you will start getting quite a few phone calls. Also this will be the time that many of the previous years' customers will want to re-employ you on a regular basis. The first lawn cut will need doing, early flowering shrubs trimmed, old bulb vegetation cleared away

May – June

First hedge cuts may be needed at this time, if you live in a student town then you may get some students that are about to leave there house and have grass that has not been cut in a year. I find that these months are the most busy of the year as everything is growing so fast so be prepared for some long days and maybe even the occasional weekend.

July – August

Things can go a little quieter now but your regular customers will still need you. Some years, if there is very little rain then you may find that your regular lawn cuts no longer need to be done but there should be plenty of other work to keep you busy

September – October

There will still be enough work in these months to easily fill your days. Leaf clearing will start to become a major part of your work and grass will still be growing. A final hedge cut is usually done around now

November – December

The daylight will start to limit just how much work you can get done and you will most likely want to have a week off over Christmas so you should have enough to fill your available time. Regular customers that don't want or need to keep you on all year round will often keep you on until December.

Gardening is obviously very seasonal work so if you can, then put in the hours over the summer and then you will not need to worry so much in the winter if there are quiet times. Any self employment will have busy and quiet times so try not to let it concern you. If it is the height of summer and you find yourself with nothing to do then you may need to look at your advertising strategy again.

Administration

Some people employ an accountant to sort out all of their financial affairs and they can be reasonably cheap for a sole trader, around £200. I do mine on my own as I don't think they are too hard to do if you are a sole trader. It is simply a matter of keeping track of all the money that goes in and out and at the end of the financial year, sending this information off to the HMRC.

I have an excel spreadsheet for each month with a column for the date, one for the amount of money that comes in, one for the source of the money i.e. the customer name, one for amount of expenditure and one for the source of each expenditure. They are then all totalled up at the bottom and the totals from each month are added up on a separate page. I have included my email at the end of the book and if you would like a copy of this template then I am happy to send it to you.

Some people may want receipts and some people will need invoicing for payment so with these, you will have a copy of the payment details but a large number of customers will simply give you cash at the end of the job so it is up to you to record this and keep track.

Anything that can be reasonably passed off as a business expense should be included in your calculations. Obviously any tools that you buy and any advertising costs should be included but there are other things that you might not consider such as suncream, stationery, rent for your garage and your home's land line.

There are some things like your house land line, your broadband and large items like a new computer that are used partly for business and partly for your private life. In these cases you will need to decide how much it is used for business and how much personal and divide it accordingly. For instance if you buy a new computer for £400 and use it 25% of the time for business and 75% for personal use, then you are entitled to claim £100.

From April to April you will need to take away the the total costs from the total income and this will give you your taxable earnings that you will need to give to HMRC for them to send you a tax bill.

When you are first starting your business then you are required to inform the HMRC that you are now doing self employed work. You can do this alongside a different regular paying job but you must tell them this. You will have a period of a few months from first starting to do this but I would advise doing it as soon as you can in case you end up forgetting.

You travel expenses are a different matter. You can claim a fixed rate for your mileage, currently around 45p per mile. This is supposed to cover all of the expenses such as petrol, insurance, tax and repairs to the car. You can instead, claim a capital allowance for the actual costs of running the car and this can include vehicle costs and repairs.

If you have not been self employed before then it may come as a shock to you to get a large tax bill once a year rather than paying some every month. You must always remember that this is coming and keep some money in the bank. There are ways that you can pay it in installments and you can find out about this from the HMRC and might be a good idea if you are not good at saving.

Check out the HMRC website as it has a lot of helpful advice and whenever I have phoned them they have also been very helpful. It may seem complex at times but they are not trying to trip you up and will offer help when you need it.

I have never bothered with a business account and for a sole trader I do not think that they are nessesary. Some banks may not like you using a personal account for business but I have never encountered this. Business accounts also have a fee attached so unless you are a limited company then there is probably no need. You will have to make sure that cheques are made out to you personally and not to your trading name as you will not be able to cash these with a personal account.

There is also no need to register for VAT and I would advise not to. If you do then you will have to charge all of your customers extra and most domestic customers will not be able to claim it back. Once your turnover reaches a certain threshold, currenly £81000 per year then you will have to register for VAT but this will probably not be an issue for a few years.

Conclusion

If you have reached this far in the book then you will hopefully still want to become a gardener and I beleive that you have made a good choice. There can be hard times but once you have started then I doubt that you will ever want to go back to being an employee.

If you have any further questions, comments on the book or some things that I have missed out then please email me and let me know at sim209@hotmail.com.

Printed in Great Britain
by Amazon